I need you to love me a little harder on the
days I feel like breaking apart.

## OTHER BOOKS BY ROBERT M. DRAKE

Spaceship (2012)

The Great Artist (2012)

Science (2013)

Beautiful Chaos (2014)

Beautiful Chaos 2 (2014)

Black Butterfly (2015)

A Brilliant Madness (2015)

Beautiful and Damned (2016)

Broken Flowers (2016)

Gravity: A Novel (2017)

Star Theory (2017)

Chaos Theory (2017)

Light Theory (2017)

Moon Theory (2017)

Dead Pop Art (2017)

Chasing The Gloom: A Novel (2017)

Moon Matrix (2018)

Seeds of Wrath (2018)

Dawn of Mayhem (2018)

The King is Dead (2018)

**For Excerpts and Updates please follow:**

Instagram.com/rmdrk
Facebook.com/rmdrk
Twitter.com/rmdrk

*ISBN: 978-1-7326900-2-8*

Book Cover: Robert M. Drake
Cover Image licensed by Shutter Stock Inc.

For The Broken.

# CONTENTS

# SEEDS OF WRATH

ROBERT M. DRAKE

## BE FUCKING KIND

Be kind.

I know it's okay
to change your mind
but for Christ's sake,
be kind.

There are two ways
things can go,
two ways things can end:

*The gentle way
or the hard way.*

And there is no reason
to choose the hard way.

If you must,
that is,
break someone

then please be kind.
Do it softly.
Do it with consideration.

Do it with fragile hands
as you would want
to be handled.

We all have a shattering point.

We all fear the same things—
cry over the same things—
die over the same things.

Let the fall
be tolerated.

And the hurting be
a little more human.

Believe me,

there is no better way
to break someone else's heart.

So please,
if you must…

*Be soft.*
*Be gentle.*

And among all,
always try

to be kind.

## YOU LET YOURSELF

You let yourself get hurt.
You let yourself feel.

You take the goddamn risk,
regardless of how it turns out.

You're living
and I don't mean
just keeping yourself alive.

You're living for yourself,
for the people you love

And I admire that about you.

You're strong for every reason
and you matter to so many people.

So, how could you
think you're weak.

When everytime you fall
you come back
stronger than before.

You're brave
and that's what makes you
so goddamn beautiful.

## BRICK HOUSE

One Saturday night,
in a bar called Brick House
in Wynwood

a guy,
a fan of mine is introduced to me.

Our mutual friend says
he's been reading my work
for the past few years
on and offline.

He says he has most
of my books,
my novel
and my poetry collections.

He goes on about
the human condition.

*"blah blah blah..."*

I'm too drunk—too sloppy
to be getting into
this type of conversation
right now,

so please excuse me.

My god,
the music clashes
toward my face,
finding its way
through the eardrums.

"You say 'sometimes'
a lot in your work.
Why is that," he asks.

It catches my attention.

Time slows.
The liquor spills.
My hand is moist
from the spillage.

"Goddamn it!" I yell.

Now my shirt is all wet.

I look at him and reply,

"Because sometimes
people hurt.

Because sometimes
people cry.

Because sometimes
people get what they want

while other times
they don't.

Because sometimes
people fall in
and out of love.

Because sometimes
you marry the wrong person
and so on.

And because,

in all honesty
nothing is certain,
not even life itself.

The only things
that are unavoidable
are death, taxes
and debt."

Everything else happens
to everyone
at least once
in their lifetime.

And sometimes,
almost too often,
but never does it

*NOT*

happen
at all.

## SIMPLE MADNESS

And the truth
we all seek
is simple

and it has taken me
years to understand—
to break down

and apply it to
my very own life.

But the truth is,

all you have to do
is love yourself.

You're enough.

Believe it.

Enough for the whole
goddamn world,

enough for the people
you love
and enough for yourself.

Believe it.

No one
but yourself
is going to see you

and believe in you

the way
you will

for yourself.

You have too much
in you
and you should
always believe.

There is no better way
to find happiness.

*No better way
to reach*

*nirvana.*

## A MESSAGE

A girl sends me a message
on the gram.

"You're a goddamn genius.
I always tell my friends
about your work," she says.

Well that's a relief

but

I'm no genius,
at least I don't think I am.

I've just been let down.
I've failed more than once.

I've been hurt several times
and I've broken others
just as hard as well.

I've been cheated on.
I've been discriminated against.
I've been singled out.

I've been cast out…
isolated, beaten
and misunderstood.

Hell!

Well if that makes me a
"Goddamn genius,"
I guess
we are a planet full of
goddamn geniuses.

And it's just a case of
who has a better way
of expressing themselves

in the end.

## WHAT YOU CAN AND CAN'T DO

You can't control
how long
someone wants to love you.

Or how long
they are willing to
stick around.

All you can do is,
learn to let go
and carry on.

When someone's heart
isn't there.

When someone's heart
isn't ready.

When someone's heart
no longer belongs to you.

When someone's heart
outgrows you.

When someone's heart
just doesn't feel the same.

All you can do is

learn to let go
and carry on.

You can't control people
but you can learn
to adapt

and accept how
things change.

## UNISON

And yes,
both men and women
are completely different beings.
One tends to need

what the other doesn't
and that's okay.

But I have learned
throughout my years,

that no matter how old
one gets.

No matter what they write about
on the paper
or air on TV,

both men
and women need love.

They need people
and they need to feel
assured,

that someone out there
needs them.

Regardless of
how they dress.

What they eat.

What they do
and don't do.

We all need someone
to go home to.

Someone to fight for
and someone who'll give
us meaning

in a meaningless
world.

## THE WAY YOU GET UP

People are going to
let you down
and there is no way
you can ever be
ready for it.

*And that is
the realist shit.*

Some people are wolves
in disguise.

They have more wrath
in them than peace.

And for reasons unknown
they always display
the biggest smiles

and have the strongest hands
to pull you in.

It's hard,
you know,
telling the difference between
friend or foe.

Between love and hate.

Between a helping hand
or a stab in the back.

So have this in mind.

Carry it
with the tenderness
in your soul,

and know
that you must go into things
with a full heart.

That yes,
you must openly love
and trust everyone you meet
but also keep your guard up.

Because people are going
to do what people do best.

Therefore,
some will love you.

Some will hate you.

But never trust
someone who is torn inbetween
because

that is one hard situation
to put yourself in.

So you should *NEVER*
trust someone
who doesn't know

what to feel.

## HOW YOU HAVE BEEN

I wonder
how you've been.

If your dreams
have been met

and

if your hands
have ever been held
as beautifully

as we held
ours.

## CONFUSED ABOUT PEOPLE

A friend of mine
is confused about people
and love.

Her heart is barely there.

Her mind is lost
and her feelings are trapped
in a wind storm.

She asks,

*"Why it is
we let people in,
even when we know
they're no good
to us?"*

I look at her and reply.

"That is what happens
when you let people in.

Most of the time
they destroy you.

They take more
than they need,

more than you can give.

*That's human nature.*

To take and take and take.

Until there's nothing left
to arouse them.

Until there's nothing left
but bones
and shattered pieces.

And sadly,
sometimes that's love.

One gives more
than the other.

One is more committed
and one eventually
has enough."

She looks at me and smiles
then cries and then smiles
again.

"You always know
what to say,"

she says.

I look her in the eyes
and my soul pierces
through her heart.

"Well, kid,
when you've been
through enough
it kind of comes out easily."

The truth flows from the soul
like dying stars looking
for new air to breathe

and rest comes down soon after.

*The truth hurts*
and there is nothing
more terrifying

than that.

## HOLD IT AGAINST YOU

You want to believe
that people
are against you.

That the whole goddamn world
is watching you
and they're rooting
for you to fall—to burn.

But no.

It is not like that.

No one really wants
to witness the pain
of another person.

No one ever
wants to see someone
they know die.

That is not built within
our human hearts
and yet,

we all cling to this kind
of trouble—this kind
of hurting.

We don't wish it
on other people
but we relate to it
and understand

the different cries
because of this ache.

So no, my friend...

people do not hate you.

People are not
talking behind your back.

People are not
looking forward
to your decline.

They're just watching you…
be yourself,
admiring you from afar
and getting prepared
to catch you…

just in case
you ever have the need
to fall.

ROBERT M. DRAKE

## THE MOLD

We are all
shaped by some
incredible sadness.

By a part of our past
that still hurts.

## ANOTHER NIGHT

*Another night drunk.*

Another lonely night
pouring myself to the paper.

I hear steps.
They stop behind me
near the door.

It is her, the devourer
of all worlds.

She interrupts me,
sometimes…

she pulls me away from
my work—from my typewriter.

She says we have a problem
and that, there is something
she's been needing to tell me.

I type a few words
before I give her my time.

I am on fire
so I don't want to lose
my juice.

I wrote a poem about
sorrow, the usual...

heartache and the gentle
touch of sweet isolation.

She stands before the door.

Bynow
I know she is serious.

She keeps waiting
and breathing hard.

I standup and frown.

"What is it? I'm working here,"
I say.

Now I don't mean to be
the way I am being
but it is moments like these

where I have found my
frequency, my momentum,
you know?

"We need to talk," she snaps
and does this hissy sound...
like a train pressing
on the breaks.

"Alright, give me a few."

"No. We need to talk
right now."

She stomps her left foot,
demanding and igniting
yet another feud.

One, that,
for the life in me
I do not want to be
a part of.

"I'm seeing someone else,"
she says in all her glory.

"We're done!"

For a moment,
I think it is a joke…

because despite our
differences I actually believed

we were forever.

"Well, that's alright,"I say.

"That's fine!" I add.

Her eyes widen,
her teeth grinding.

And my god,
if you look close enough
you can almost see
the steam rising from the top
of her skull.

"That's all you have
to say to me?"

"Yep,"

I say as I tumble
back toward my seat
to attend to my work.

"Just make sure to close
the door."

I wave my hand as I begin
to type.

I am distorted
and confused.

She storms out
and the color of rage
fills my mind.

I never saw her
after that night.

And all this time
I thought it was a joke,
a cruel little mind game,
we, too, often
would play on one another.

She broke my heart
that night, man…

but I was so drunk
and later, so high
that the pain I felt

prevented me from crying.

From showing
any kind of emotion.

It didn't let me
shatter properly.

It just helped me
hold it in.

That was in the late '90s

and I've been holding
it in since...

at least, I think I have.

It is no wonder
why no other woman

has been able to capture
my heart
the way she did.

She made me laugh
and I took her for granted…

and it is a shame
that I never took the time
to realize this...

not until…

now.

## VALIDATION 3

We all need someone
to validate
our lives—our existence.

It's the only reason
left to go on.

*For the people you love.*
*For our friends and family.*
*For our sons and daughters.*

They give our lives meaning.

And yes,
we must learn to live
for ourselves

but we must also learn
to live for those
we need the most.

And we must never forget this.

We must always remember
how much
we need the people we love

and how important

it is to let them know
how they make

us feel.

## TWO MONTHS

We were together
for two months.

She said,
those were probably
the best two months

of her life and mine,
too.

I don't know how
things fell apart
or where they began to.

But it is not like it matters.

Now,
almost twenty years later,

I still think about her
and our young,
naive love.

Our unblossomed love.

And we loved,
by all means,

that is the only way
to describe it.

Although
we were children,

we loved the way
people love.

Close and together…
without guidance
and without any kind of rules.

Arguing over nothing…
wasting our lives in the stream
of broken love.

We were young, too young.

We didn't know any better
but still,

there are some things
in life that come naturally.

Like the way we would run
toward each other
after a long day.

Like the way we used to
talk on the phone for hours

after school.

Like the way we used
every minute doing something.

Figuring out something.

Twenty years later,
I still think about her
and she probably
still thinks about me.

Unblossomed
wilted and uprooted.

We were each other's
flowers

and sadly,

we were both picked
by the wrong hands.

But it is not like it matters.

We have different lives now.

Different ideas
goals
and dreams.

And it is a shame,

that every day we wake up
in our very different lives

but wonder

what it would be like
if our lives would have

never parted ways.

There are some people
in this world who are
born to be loved.

But there are also some
who are born to be missed.

And I miss you.

I miss you. I miss you.

I am glad to have met you.

Amen.

## SECRETS

You still have
a lot of time.

A lot of choices to make.

There is no need
to rush through your life—
to go through moments
without breathing.

Without inhaling people.

The ones who bring out
the best in you.

There's still time for you—
to be who you want to be.

To feel what you want to feel

and

to spend your time
with those who matter most.

There's still a fight in you
and there's still enough of it
to overcome

anything life throws at you.

You have so much
to look forward to.

So much light
despite the darkness
that flows

*everywhere.*

There's still so much to do.

So much inspiration to be found.

So many people to love,
and hold on to a little bit longer
than usual.

There's still so much time.
More than enough.
Don't waste it on pointless,
trivial things.

There's so much ahead
and I just want you
to be a lover of things

of people
of moments
of life.

And I want you
to take as much of it
as you can.

So you can give
people the hope
they need

everywhere
you go.

## FREE WORLD

Most people don't care
about other people's
opinions anymore.

We live in a free world,
baby.

In an age when people
want to think for themselves.

When people are sick
and tired of being told
what to feel.

*What to love.*
*What to hate.*

But no one cares.

We live in an age
where we all have access
to information

and on the tip
of our fingers, too.

But I understand.

You want to state your opinion,
one no one cares about.

It is sad. *It really is.*

That you believe by sharing it
is enough for you to feel
as if you're connected

to someone—to anyone
who's willing to acknowledge you.

But people don't care.

No one does.

Especially when it's hateful shit.

Hateful shit
on someone else's art.

On someone else's
demise
or downfall.

*No one cares.*
*No one cares.*
*No one cares.*

So why put so much energy
into it?

Why hold your breath
for that long?

It makes no sense
to keep feeding beasts
that aren't there.

People are tired.

People have been through enough.

Too much discrimination
being thrown at them
throughout their daily lives.

And you think they want to
read more negativity?

You're a fool,

and hate doesn't move people.

Empty words
do not matter.

Fire beneath rain
cannot survive or strive.

You're a fool
if you believe
people will follow

a blind leader.

If people will follow
someone who lacks truth.

And I say truth
because if you spoke of truth,

you would understand
how destruction doesn't
support life.

How people who've been
through hell only want
to walk through heaven.

And hell is hot.
And hell is heavy.
And hell is a place
most of us have been through.

But only those
who have yet
to feel the burn of life—
of true struggle

speak of hate.
Share hate.

Because around here,
hate is a word we use

for those who haven't
lived enough—

for those who haven't
graduated from the struggle.

And love is an action,
a weapon we use to fight—
to bring them back
where they belong.

Love fiercely, my people.

Love hard.

And never forget to
always choose it,
despite the hate that surrounds us.

It is the only way
we could recognize

those who have been through enough
and those who

have barely lived
at all.

## REPEAT

It has been beautifully said
time and time again.

That when you belong to someone,
you belong to someone.

And since I could remember,
I've belonged to you.

No matter how far I go,
I am yours.

No matter how far you go,
you are mine.

And we belong together,
no matter how hard

we want to believe
that we don't.

This is why
we keep finding each other,

the way we keep finding
each other.

There's no other way

to explain this kind

of phenomenon
other than love.

## THE URGE

I urge my brothers
and sisters to be better.

To make soft poems
of tragic, ugly things.

To find figments of light
in the darkest hearts.

And to fight the labels
that don't represent us
the best way they can.

I urge all of you
to find your perfect truth.

To find what speaks to you…
what comforts you,

to understand it—master it,
and then to pass it on
to someone in need.

I urge this of you,
my sweet people.

I want this from you
because you should want

this for yourselves.

To find peace and love
your way, and to exhale it

the same way you let it in.

One love.

## MY BROTHER HEX

My brother, Hex
and I are at the international mall
waiting
for a mutual friend of ours.

This is sometime in 2001,
long before the revitalization
of poetry online.

We have the usual conversation:

*Lost women,*
*lost money,*
*lost people*
*and our lost childhoods.*

A shift in the air arises.

"Man, Bobby,
why do you even write poetry?
 It's been dead
since the Beats."

He has a point.

Perhaps
poetry has been dead…
long dead.

No one is talking about it.
No one is buying the books
as they once were.

It has become a niche now.
It's been long forgotten,

perhaps since I was born—
dead even, who knows.

"I don't know.
It's just one of those things
I feel I have to do,
you know?

*I just do it.*

Not for anyone else
but myself."

He takes a sip of his cola
and swallows it.

"Yeah but don't you feel
you can be using your time
doing other things?

You paint
and make clay sculptures.

You should focus on that more.
There could be a market for it,"

he says.

This is what most people
don't understand.

The creators.
The influencers.
The peacemakers.
The healers.
The fighters.

The ones who want to
change the world.

They never do
what they do
over a check.

They never come into their movement
thinking they're going to get rich.

*They do what they do
because they must.*

Because if they don't

the world wouldn't
make much sense…

and because making art,
saving people—healing people

and making a difference

is the only way
they know how to live.

Some people are born
to serve their people.

Whether it is through art.
Through poetry.
Through music.
Through films.

Some people are meant
to save other people...

no matter what practice they use
or don't use...

long before
they are even born.

## OPEN MYSELF TO YOU

It is 1:42 a.m. right now.

I am here lying on my bed,
typing, thinking, wondering
if everything I've every done
has been the right thing.

*This is the time*
*I open up to myself.*

When I confess and look
back at all the things I did,

the things I didn't do,
and the things I regret most.

For reasons unknown,
I always tend to get myself
stranded in my regrets.

They have me dreaming,
swimming in a puddle
of things I should have done.

I have too many to list.
Too many people I've hurt
too many things I've let
pass me by.

Perhaps, I am naive
or naive enough to believe…

that one day
I'll get a second chance.

That everything happens
for a reason.

Regardless
of how it ends.

This is the piece of me
I do not like.

The regrets that cause
mental breakdowns,

heart palpitations
and heavy breathing

as if I'm inhaling
through a straw.

People don't seem to understand
what I feel.

My dead brother's
prayers are with me
and the demons
he took with him

surround the walls.

It's dark.
It's cold.

I hear a mild hum
coming from my fan.
It plays through my ears.

I could have died,
I say to myself.

Maybe I should have.
Who knows…

because every night
I think about him.

I could have saved you,
my little brother.

I could have
talked you out of it.

But the night you called
I was being selfish.

And now,
almost always,
I contemplate…

why do people do
the things they do?

Things they regret later…

to live their lives
being haunted by
what could have been done.

And I regret ignoring you, brother.
I regret thinking you were
fucking around—that this was
just another phase in your life.

But I was wrong
and you are gone.

And now,
I am just another man
with a brain full of regrets

and a heart full
of empty rooms.

## SO MANY PEOPLE

I've met so many people
in my life,
a thousand or even more,

but none of them
have ever made me feel
what you've made me feel.

And I'm not talking about love
or the idea of it.

I'm talking about life.
About noticing everything
and breaking it down
in details.

When I'm with you,
every atom in my body
is alive.

Every thought
gets fired straight toward
the universe

like a beam of light
rushing to get through
the darkness.

You give me life,
my sweet girl.

You have saved me
without even knowing it.

All I can hope is,
that one day,

you find someone
who can do the same.

Find a thousand names.
A thousand lives.
A thousand stories and faces.

Find them.
Search for them.

And know
that there will only be
one person
who can bring you peace.

Only one person who
can give you all the reasons
you need to stay alive.

To *continue* to live.

This is what I want for you,

and your sister, forever.

Life forever.
Love forever.

Understanding
and friendship

forever…

I want the both of you
to meet people.

To not be afraid of them.

To be kind to them
and to believe,
that one day,

you will finally understand
what I am writing about

and you will finally understand
what it was
that I felt

the moment I first held you
in my arms.

## BURIED MEMORIES

I don't know
why people bury
what they bury.

And I don't know
why good people
sometimes
make bad choices.

And I've made enough of them
to admit
when I was wrong.

If this is the only way
I know how to say sorry

then by all means,
let me write it.

Let the truth flow out of me.
like open wounds
expelling crimson waves
of pain.

This is my sorrow
and it is true.

It is heavy,

dark and away
from the bright sun.

I keep it beneath me,
beating,
pumping sadness into me.

Feeding me
through tubes
as my body sinks into my bed.

Dwelling into my past
like replayed memories
reminding me over
and over and over

of the way I extinguished
your sun.

This is hard for me,
but this is the only way
I know how to say,
I'm sorry.

To write hurting words.

To cry a little between
the spaces, between the letters
and pauses.

Shit it *hurts* that I hurt you.

I'm sorry, kid,
I really am.

For all the trouble
I've caused you.

For the coward lies
I've told
and the careless words
I've let spring out of my lips.

Like hollow points
slamming against a concrete wall.

I'm sorry and I love you.

It's just hard for me
to be honest in front of you.

So take this letter
under consideration
and please acknowledge
that

I was wrong,

and how I now feel
like a river, slowly passing through.
like breeze with nowhere to go.

I love you.

I miss you.

And sadly, this letter,
will never reach you...

because I, myself,
do not know
where to send it.

Because

I am too late.

always.

# FULL OF LOVE OR HATE

I blame my daughters.
They have turned me into
a sensitive man.

*Either full of love*
*or full of hate.*

I feel things now
with the same intensity
of a dying star.

They flame my sky
and all I see are fireballs
soaring through the darkness.

This is my life
and these are the years
I've gone through.

And before the kiddos
I couldn't see properly.

I couldn't feel.
I couldn't appreciate.

I couldn't understand
the value of other people.

I blame my daughters,
my sweet babies.

They have lifted everything
that has ever weighed
me down.

And they have given me
a second chance.

At love,
at trust
and friendship.

And I can never repay them
for what they've done.

I will spend my entire life
thanking them...

my entire existence
is testament for all you have both
brought back to my life.

Knowing this,

has given me great joy
but also

great sorrow.

## THESE LABELS, MAN

Labels are for
the shirts we wear
and for the pants we
put on.

They're not for people.

They're not for the things
you do
and believe in—for what
you feel.

And it's the same
with false imagery
and what's real.

You don't have to pretend
to be someone you're not
to *feel* wanted.

You don't have to act
a certain way
or say certain things
to be loved.

And for Christ's sake,
just be yourself.

Let every scar
on your skin.

Every flaw
in your personality
genuinely surface.

And I know
it's easier said
than done.

Therefore,
this kind of practice
doesn't have to happen
overnight
or the next day.

You have to
take your time.

Stop comparing yourself
to other people
and kill the labels.

They do not represent you
or us, for that matter.

Let them burn.

They are ultimately
the great demise

of our youth.

The slaying of our self-growth
and the murder of identity

in the new world.

## IS IT THAT BAD?

Is it so bad to say
that although
I am a man

I am soft inside
and I care about others?

Is it so bad to say
I love you?

To hold it within
because I am afraid
of what might happen next.

Is it so bad to say
that sometimes I cry?

That sometimes I hurt.

That sometimes
I feel so goddamn alone.

Is it so bad to say
that I am comfortable
being myself
and sometimes I am not?

That being such a way

doesn't mean
I've lost a part of who I am.

A part of who I want
to become.

Is it so bad? *Is it?*

To treat people equally
for the way they speak—
for the way they live,
think and feel.

For the way they treat
other people.

Is it so bad to be a man,
a sensitive man,
a sensitive human
but still be strong

enough to carry
the weight of the world
on my shoulders?

Who feels more
than he should and
feels more broken
as time passes by.

Is it so bad

to want to do something
about the way we really

see each other
and about the way
we don't?

Is it so bad to want change?

To want to be treated
in such a way
that you treat others
when no one is watching.

Is it evil of me to care?

To be human enough
to deeply feel pain when I see
others in despair.

Is it just me?
Am I alone in this?

To have this burning hope
of freedom—of respect
and understanding.

To live a certain way,
to be what I believe in.

To use my words to build

bridges and not walls.

Is it so bad to be kind
to one another.

Is it so hard to be kind
to one another,
my sweet people.

*Is it?*

## CARRY THIS FOR YOU

And now

deep down inside,
I'll always carry
something for you

because you made me feel
a certain way.

You made the familiar
feel unfamiliar
and the unfamiliar
feel

as if

it's been with me
all along.

# THE SAME

Are we not the same?

Do we not cry the same tears?
Do we not feel the same pain?

The same burning sensation
that thrives from the center

of our souls
when the heart is broken?

Do we not
lie about the same things?

Try to hide the parts
of ourselves we don't love?

Are we not
both fragile at times?

Insecure about our flaws

and

do we not
soak all over our emotions
when we feel scared?

Do we not fight
the same evil?
Stand for the same struggle:

*One that's been
too hard to ignore.*

Then my god,
why is it that you want
to be better?

When all this time
you've been fighting
to stand beside us,

to be respected
and loved
in the same light.

I'm here with you, my people.

My sisters.
My brothers.

I am here with you.

Fighting with you.
Believing with you.

Hurting with you,
and dreaming of better days

with you.
I am here,
my sweet people.

Going through
the same problems.

Getting pushed
while pushing back at the sun.

At the waves that drown us
at the same pace.

We are *the same*.

There is no him or her.

We are the same
and we are all restrained,

tyrannized
and victimized

by the same system.

There is no difference.

The pain is authentic
and the tears are real

and the way we share

what hurts

is forever

the same.

# CHOOSE LOVE, FOREVER

Choose love, forever,
my sweet people.

The love of self.

The love of good company—
of good health
and of good wine.

Choose love, forever,
my sweet people.

Over hate,
over self-doubt
and criticism of neighbor—
choose love.

Choose love, forever,
my sweet people.

Over confusion,
manipulation and the
corruption of man
and woman.

Choose love, always love.

I wouldn't spend

much time
doing anything
else.

## IT NEVER ENDS

Sometimes
you love someone so much
that it never really ends.

What they made you feel
never quite goes away.

It just sort of stays,

somewhere lingering...

in the backs of our brains
and hearts...

where it *always* hurts
the most.

## THIS POEM...

This poem is about
my depression...

I don't know
how to start this
and I don't know
how to end it either.

But most times
I feel as if my life
is crumbling.

Most times
I feel as if I haven't grown
at all.

As if I haven't
gone through enough.

As if all the pain I've felt
has been for nothing
or has been for everything.

I don't know why,
that is,

why this deep sense
of failure and nothingness

fills me.

I don't know why
I expect so much more

or why I behave
the way I behave—
feel the way I feel

and lose my mind
and heart in the middle of it all.

These are the nights
I find who I am.

And even though
I have everything I need,

in so many ways,
I still feel empty.

I still carry this hollow void
that is heavier
than most could even
begin to imagine.

or so I think.

I cannot move.

I cannot breathe

and sometimes
every atom in my being cries.

The tears fill to the tip
of my space

and

I drown over the things I love—
over the things I don't love.

Over the people I love
and don't love.

I fall and break
in the softest way—
in the quietest way.

And no one ever hears
the shattering of my soul.

The silent weep
that crawls out of my heart
at night.

No one ever knows
what to say.

No one ever knows what to feel

what to think...

when I reveal a little bit
of this sorrow.

It follows me.

It flows within me.
It stirs me and pulls me
toward the darkness.

The soul is filled with
colorless hues.

And everytime I learn to let go,
it comes back.

It reminds me how
it will never leave me.

How it needs me to survive.

It feeds off my light
and it is never thankful
for what it takes.

This pain.
This hurt.
This longing to feel free.

I sometimes believe
I was put on this Earth

to cry.

To die in soft hands
and to rise
right before dawn.

Everything seems to make sense
right when it finds its end.

Everything that hurts,
almost, always,
makes me feel at home.

In a strange way
it makes me who I am.

And in a strange way

I am thankful to it

for gently bringing me
back to Earth…

everytime I feel

as if

I no longer
want to be here

at all.

## IT MUST BE LOVE

It must be love.

Broken, confused,
mutilated love.

But it's love.

Raw and full
of both happiness
and pain.

Blossoming into something
none of us understand.

If it hurts,
why do we cling
to it even more?

Why do we stay
when we know
how it ends most nights.

We return to one another
leaving trails full of tears

to again find our way
when we both feel lost.

You're my home
and I am yours.

Broken, confused,
mutilated love.

But it's love, nonetheless.

*Our love.*

Crazy, young, rebellious.

We love.
We live.
We laugh
and we cry.

This must be
what it feels like

to drown

without being submerged
in water.

## PLATFORM

And now we have built
our own platform.

A platform we created,
one we control.

And now many of us
have formed lives, careers
from this platform.

And now all is well.
All is at peace.

And now come the companies,
the thirsty, devilish, money hungry
companies.

To dilute what we've created.

To manipulate
our young minds
and hearts

and try to sell us their
manufactured dream.

This fuckery.
This grand scam.

They write contracts
and give us a little piece
of OUR souls back.

A little piece
of what *WE'VE* already
created.

There you go.

Here is a small advance
a small percentage of your own art

and your word that you will
NEVER speak
against them—god forbid that.

They steal your creation
and smile.

Let us be friends
as long as we own your pain
and monetize from it.

Nothing is certain.

Nothing is free
not even our own thoughts.

Young writers,
this you must take with you.

Everytime you sell
your manuscript

to a publisher
for an advance,

you lose a little part
of your soul.

And you should never
sell your heart—your pain.

Your soul
is worth so much more
than that.

## MAGNITUDE

Every person you meet
will change you,
but not all of them will have

the same magnitude
or significance.

Not all of them
will move you
or touch your soul,

and not all of them
will meet your expectations.

Like I said,

you will meet hundreds of people
during your lifetime

and some you will remember
while others
you will forget.

But only one will conquer
your heart the way it was meant
to be tamed.

Only one will hold you

in the softest of ways,
and only one will make you
appreciate your memories…

your scars…

your mistakes
and your flaws

forever.

## SOME GOOD

My god,
I am just trying
to do some good,

be good,
you know?

I'm trying to change
my life
and change the lives
of those around me.

But why are there so many
devils around me?

Why am I tempted
in the worst of ways?

Why am I beaten down,
exiled and betrayed…

the way I am?

My god, I'm tired.

My heart aches.

My bones drowning

with the blood of my past.

With sin and pain
of my future.

My god, I'm so tired.

Is this a test of judgement?
A test of moral?
Λ test of my endurance?

Of what I should be doing
and what I shouldn't?

The devil's waltz
beneath my chest.

Beneath my Earth
beneath my ocean
and spread

through air like
the scent of war
and death.

My god,
why is it so hard
being human?

Why can't it all
be so simple?

Why can't we all
leave some things behind.

Why can't we all
let go of the trivial things.

The things that do too little
to save humanity.

To save the steam
you need to save yourself.

My god,
please let me be understood.

Please let me do some good.

Please let me be true
to myself
and what I stand for.

Let me be prepared.

Let me be ready for
whatever comes next.

For the people in my life
for the people who deserve
my perfect flame.

My god,

I am just trying
to do
some good, you know?

I'm trying.

My god, let me be.

Let other people understand this.

That what I am
is all I am
and there is
no other way to be.

Just let me be.

Let me try.
Let me fail.
Let me succeed.

Let me raise myself high
and let me fall
when the time comes.

I'm just trying to do some good
but my god,

there are so many devils
telling me otherwise—
hiding me from the truth,

and too little angels
guiding me down the right path.

I am lost, but I am still trying
to do some good...

no matter what,

and

I am searching
for more than just flesh.

For more than just a shoulder
to lean on—for more
than someone to relate to.

My god,

I inhale solitude,
exhale hope,
and pray,

that maybe one day,
you'll have mercy on
my soul.

## IT HURTS

It hurts
because you've been
surrounded by people
so long

that you've forgotten
how to listen
to your own voice.

And you've been so concerned
with the feelings of others

that you barely know
who you are—what you've become.

But don't lose yourself
in the transition.

This is something
we've all gone through.

So don't feel too badly
for it.

You just need to know
what being alone feels like.

What listening to what

you feel
is like.

And believe me
it takes time—lots of it,
an abundance of seconds
and hours.

But everything you need
is being spoken into the dawn
of the universe.

All you have to do is
isolate yourself,
breathe and listen.

Sometimes
time and being alone
is a remedy to all things

that hurt.

## MINDS AHEAD

It is not
that people
read other people's

minds
or live in other people's
brains.

It is just
that all of us,
sooner or later,
go through the same ordeal.

The same tragedies.

People relate through pain,
through sorrow
and tears.

*Human suffering is relative.*

And if our hearts remain open,
maybe one day
we'll all
be able to understand,

how all of us
have different pains

and different cries.
But when it's all
said and done...

when we hurt,
we all bleed

and slowly dissolve
the same way.

## IT GETS BETTER

You're never
going to get better.

What I carry
deep within my brain
is a disease.

I remember too much.
I forget too much.

*Too many* little things
I should know.

The mind goes backwards.

The slur of words
and the lack of focus
wrap around me
like a belt.

Like a heavy,
terrible,
old belt.

If I said it one day,
I'll lose track of it
the next.

The mind is elastic.

A rubber band that shoots
darts into the wild,

into the dark,
the nothingness
of man's heart.

I do not expect you,
the reader, to understand this.

But the more I write
the more I feel
like I am losing myself.

As if these words
carry my soul

and they are all
on borrowed time.

I don't have enough
I'll never have enough.

Time is a slow
burning candle
too far to see.

Sooner or later
I'll run out.

I'll forget—
even my words—
what I feel.

My heart—
how it beats
and my mind—

how the thoughts
lose their way
off the rusted rails.

I fear
how sooner or later
the people

I love will no longer
be able to find me.

Will no longer be able
to see my soul
pouring from my pupils.

I write these words,
not only to remind you

that I will always be here
some way, somehow.

I write these words
knowing

that one day
I will no longer

have any more words
to describe how I feel.

I write these words,
these small
little dull words

For my sweet daughters.

For the two
who will always have
my heart.

Read what I've
left you two behind

and understand
how one day

I will physically be gone

but also
how on that day,

I will find my home,
snuck
within your hearts
forever.

## LIVE WITHOUT

It will always be
about the people
you can't live without

but also,
it will always be
about you.

Actually,
mostly about you.

About the way
you handle your heart,
if you followed it
or if you let it slip away.

It will always be
about you. Remember that—
hold that to the very ends
of the Earth.

And know who you want
to let into your life
and how everything affects you,
how everything happens
because of you,
regardless of how much advice
you've taken in.

Regardless
of how many times
you've played the scenario
in your mind.

Regardless
of how you see your future
or how hard it is
to move on from your past,

it will always be
about you.

The universe expands.
The Earth spins
and all you should do
is learn
how to appreciate yourself.

How to respect yourself
especially when you know
you're wrong.

Because it will always be
about you.

About you and the people
you love
and the people you failed
to love.

Beautiful and flawed
beautiful and damned.

My sweet human,
it will always be
about you.

Never forget that,
I hope.

# FIND YOU (WHO KNOWS)

And I hope you're well.

I hope you're happy,
really happy,
and I hope that someday,

one day,
you find yourself thinking
about me in the same tone.

I hope we find each other
again
and I hope we're laughing—
sharing memories

about that one time
we almost made it

but ended up
breaking each other's
hearts.

## NO FUTURE BUT STILL HOPE

I do not know
the future.

I am sorry.
I cannot see that far
but I will tell you this.

I will be there for you
until whatever happens
next.

Because right now
I feel as if nothing matters
when I am with you.

*Not the past
or the future.*

Not anything, really.

And right now,
I just want to run away
with you.

Leave it all behind,
you know?

I feel like I want to wake up

every morning
not knowing
or caring

what I'm going to do
or how my day is going
to end.

Sweetheart,
in all honesty,

I want my life to be a doorway
that'll always lead me back
to you.

No matter how far
we stray from one another.

No matter how badly
it hurts.

No matter how hard
we fight or don't.

I want my path to always
cross with yours.

So that five,
ten or maybe even twenty years
down the line...

I can look back at what
we once had and say:

*"I gave you
the best parts of me*

*and*

*because of you
I am still alive."*

## WHAT YOU FEEL

The same way you feel love
before you lose it.

The same way you finally realize
someone's worth before they're gone.

The same way you learn
how trust again

after you've been let down
a few times.

Learn to appreciate everything.

Learn to complain less—
to look for the horrors
in people less.

Learn to adapt to change—
to adapt when people
have different points of view.

Learn to accept things
as they are—to accept yourself
as you come.

Learn to view the world.
Learn to view people,

both their victories
and tragedies.

Learn, learn…
and learn some more.

But only from experience,
only from pain—from hurt.

Only from love, from joy
and all moments in-between.

Learn, and never stop learning.

Not until
your real self
reveals itself

and even so,
keep going.

*Keep learning.*
*Keep growing.*
*Keep moving forward.*

Until your bones become brittle
and your body loses its soul.

Until what breaks you
no longer breaks you.

Until everything you've learned,
and felt
comes back to you to remind you
of how far you've gone.

Of how *human you are.*

Learn, and never stop,
I beg this of you.

It is, ultimately,

the only say we have left.

The only power we still have.

Not doing so
is a massacre to the soul.

## CONTRADICTIONS

I have convictions,
contradictions…

shame,
pain
and a few things
I can't erase.

I have my own problems,
my own issues,
my own scars

and other things
I wish I could replace.

I am drunk in love
with life.

Drunk in love
with people,

both known
and unknown.

With both who are here
and no longer here.

Alone most nights

I am drowning in things
I should have done—
in things
I could have said.

I have flaws, too many.

My heart is broken
filled to the rim with regrets.

If it is one regret,
I fully regret as I sit here
in front of my typewriter

then it is this...

it is not telling you
how much I love you.

It is not telling you
how much I miss you.

How much I always cared,
despite the space

we had growing between us
throughout the years.

My sweet little brother,
kind and soft.

Sad and always in doubt.

You always wanted
to take your life away.

You always knew
you would die young

and I, too, knew this.
Yet as much as I knew...

I still let it happen.

*We ALL let it happen.*

This aches my core, my brother.

This eats me alive.
It pulls me back
into the darkness
where no light is found.

I can't erase what happened.
I can't write this pain away either.

This is why it hurts
the way it hurts.

Why blood is not needed
for old wounds to bleed.

My soul breaks
and my body is just
another vessel of pain.

A harbor of it.
A good friend of it.

I could have saved you,
my brother.

I could have.

If only I had picked up
the phone that one night
you called me...

Then perhaps,
I wouldn't be here
writing this verse.

Drunk in pain
and drunk in regret.

This is my conviction,
my sweet little brother,

and I am just as guilty
as you are
for not doing anything

and for not

trusting my gut…

when I knew
you were in so much pain.

I haven't seen the sun since,
my sweet brother,

you took it with you,
and that's what hurts
the most.

The darkness haunts me
and there will never be
another person like you.

because...

there never was.

## EASY ON YOURSELF

Go easy on yourself.

Ride into the burning sun
and walk into the mouth

of darkness
with your head held high.

Because none of this
is easy
and none of it
is supposed to be.

*Life is hard.*
*Love is hard.*
*People are hard.*
*Grief is hard.*

Letting go
and letting in is hard
goddamn,
even self-love is hard.

And learning new things
about yourself is, too.

So please,
be kind to yourself:

To your mind,
body and soul.

Be easy on yourself
and take time on yourself.

And remember,

you don't have to please everyone
and you don't have to change
for anyone either.

You just have to be okay
with who you are
and know,

that mistakes are bound to happen.

You're not meant to be perfect
and you have your whole life

to realize

how true this is...

## MY HOMEGIRL

Listening to Nas's illmatic album,
one of my favorite albums
of all time.

My homegirl, Stephanie,
has been pressing me lately.

She's been wanting to help me,
cure me
as if I was sick.

And maybe I am, who knows.

"How long are you going to be
miserable?" she asks.

I tell her
to let me be
as I am.

That it is the only way
I know how to be.

Now, I know
she wants to *"help me."*

I know
she wants to see me better

but I've only known her
for a few months

and I've been this
way my entire life.

So she's kind of an asshole
for thinking
she can change

the way I feel
in a matter of weeks—
months.

This is my life,
goddammit!

These are my feelings
and this is
the way I look at the world
from within.

It is all I know.
It is all I'll ever be.

I inhale smoke
as I isolate myself
from her.

I grab my thoughts
and take a few steps back.

"Perhaps,
in another world,
young sweet girl,

you will change me
or feel as if
you have saved me,"

I whisper to her as I leave.

Later that night
alone and tipsy
off the vodka,

I kept thinking about what
she said…

and I couldn't help
but think that
this is the way I am.

I could die today
and be forgotten tomorrow

but for Christ's sake,

please don't force change
upon me.

Don't assume
that I am miserable

because I like to spend
most of my nights alone.

Because I am a man
of few words.

This is me,
and I've been trying
to make something of myself.

I've been trying
to make myself happy
the best way I know how.

And I'm just trying
to tell my story—
my unholy truth.

Miserable or not,
*this is me...*

and most
won't understand that,

they'll just try to save you

as if
you've asked them
for the help
they *think*
you desperately need.

My people, please…

let others live.

Just be there for them
and don't try to press
your way of living upon them.

Just be there for them
and let them be free.

That is enough to save
someone's world.

## I FIND IT CRAZY

I find it crazy
that you don't talk about
what you deserve more.

That you don't speak
your greatness into existence.

It's crazy, you know?

That you complain more.
That you start your week
in the middle of a storm.

And that you don't
see the goodness
around you
but focus on the bad.

Shit, man...

Where's the hope?
Where's the sunlight?
The love?

We are all looking for it.

We are all in darkness
and it's beginning to feel

a little too cold.

Goddamn, man,
if this isn't the truth,
I don't know what it is.

But sweetheart, c'mon,
you've got to look past it—
overcome it.

You know,
the fire…
the horrors—the nightmares
of reality.

Of solitude.
Of drowning.

Of not believing
in yourself.

Of not wanting more
out of your own life
and the people around you.

Shit, man.

It's just crazy, you know?

You have so much
to look forward to,

too much ahead of you.

Everything that means
something to you
is before you…

in your grasp
but only if you want it…

*really want it.*

The oppression is real
and the death
of freedom is real.

But we have to rise
above it, slowly.

We have to inspire one another
push one another.

We have to
because *we must.*

Because there is no other way
to let go.

No other way to forgive,
to heal and above all,

no other way to love.

It's important for us
to celebrate what we have.

To appreciate what we can be
and never forget
what we've been through.

Find your peace…

in freedom.

In justice.
In equality.
In love.
In friendship.
In respect
and more.

This is what you deserve.

This is what…
we all deserve.

*There is no other way*
*to receive.*

## EXCUSE ME

Please, excuse my language
but there are some things
I must get off my chest.

Some things about the media.
Some things about our lives.
Some things about the freedom
we no longer abide by.

The rules have been altered.
Our lives have been machined.

Our dreams have been designed,
and our choices have been
isolated from our brains.

And then,
they wonder why we kill ourselves.

Why we kill our brothers
and sisters.

They wonder why we mistreat one another
over trivial things.

I inhale the yellow smoke
and reply with the fabric of pain
over my head.

Take it all in,
my sweet people,

but

*how the fuck*
do they expect us
to change the world

when they haven't given us
the tools to save ourselves.

How the fuck
do they expect us
to express ourselves

when they haven't taken the time
to teach us
how to look from within.

How to put words together
and string them
from the depths of our souls.

How the fuck
do they expect us
to love
when they haven't shown us
a thing about compassion,

a thing about risk—a thing

about losing someone
you truly,
completely, care about.

How the fuck
do they expect us
to trust
when they haven't shown us

how to break apart—to give our pieces
to strangers.

To people we have yet
to know.

To people
we could possibly
have the opportunity to love.

How the fuck
do they expect us
to not go mad
when they haven't shown us

how to control our inner moonlight,
our inner rage.

Our inner voice—thoughts
and whatever we have left
that they haven't exploited.

*How the fuck!*

This is what I ask
and this is how I answer.

The yellow smoke clears
above my skull—it vanishes
without warning.

How the fuck
can we be ourselves,
who we want to be...

when all they do
is tell us
who we should be.

Pointing out our flaws.

Monetizing off our weaknesses
and making us believe
how

all that we are
is not beautiful enough
to be loved.

To be held up high
toward the stars—
with the gods.

How the fuck, my sweet
brothers and sisters.

How the fuck can we live?
How the fuck can we be better?

How the fuck can we raise
our children—leaving goodness
behind for future generations
to come?

When everything around us
is designed to weigh us down.

To... to... make us feel
less important
and grant us the
doubt of self-love.

The doubt
of believing in one's self
and knowing
how we are all
capable of so much more.

But how the fuck, man?

How can we rise
in pot full of lies?

In a tunnel

with no light to follow.

They don't give a shit.
The ones who enslave us,

the ones who put us in debt.

The insurances
that smile
and stab us in the back.

The ones who know
our names
but not what's within
our hearts.

How the fuck can I live,
grow old and enjoy my time
on this Earth...

The self-esteem leaks out.
The self-doubt leaks out.
The self-hate leaks out.

It piles in the middle
of the avenue.

And the radio plays...
and the internet streams...
and the television is on...

and the fear clings on my shoulder

and my two-year-old daughter
is playing, laughing
without the slightest idea
of how cold the world is...

I inhale the yellow smoke

and whisper,

*"How the fuck?"*

as I look for other ways...
better ways...

to survive.

To live.

## APART FROM ME

And I hope you find more
than just yourself.

I hope you find it in you
not to hurt the people
you love,

not to put yourself down
when you feel like
breaking apart.

I hope you find miracles...
the kind that will make you
believe in love again,
in trust again...

in people and in magic...
again.

I hope these things for you,
although

we both know
we are not meant to be together...

I still
want to see you shine.

I still
want someone
to hold your hand,
even if it's not mine.

Because they deserve to be held
when you feel most alone.
To be reminded

of how beautiful
life can be.

These are the things
I want for you.

And although,
I might not be there
to witness it...

I still believe these things
will happen to you.

Because

you deserve it, kid...
with or without me.

You deserve someone
to go home to,
a place to shelter you
when it rains.

Someone to run to
when you feel vulnerable,

someone who understands,
you know?

You deserve to be loved
in all places,

especially

where you least expect it.

Word.

## THEY WANT TO

You see,
the truth about people
isn't very hard
to understand.

The ones who stay,
stay because
they want to.

Because they feel
the need to.

Because they care
and don't want to see
you alone.

They'll always be there
for you

and you never have to ask
them why.

While the ones who leave,
leave because they must.

Because they received
what they wanted
from you.

Because they no longer
see the need
in having you around.

And almost always,
they leave unexpectedly.

It's sad
but you see,

the truth about people
is simple.

You should always
admire the ones who stay
and learn
from the ones who leave...

and let your heart
and time

decide which of the two

is worth
remembering.

# IN THE WORLD

I met the strongest kid
in the world today.

We're on the same soul train.

On the same train of thought
and I was blessed to have met him.

I woke up late,
around noon.

I got dressed.
I brushed my teeth
and jumped in my car.

It was a Saturday
and I was going to go
to South Beach,

where I did most of my
jogging—thinking.

From the time I got there,
I began to suffer
from a bag of bad luck.

I sat in traffic for over two hours.
The parking took another hour.

I couldn't settle
because there were too many people
on the beach.

I forgot to charge my cellphone
the night before.

I left my wallet in my car.

(My car was parked
about half a mile away.)

And my shoelaces
kept unfastening

with almost every step
I took
as I ran.

My blood was boiling.
I stopped and yelled,

*"Fuck!"*

as my shoe fell off my foot.

I was almost done with my jogging.
I was running on the boardwalk.

The whole time I couldn't think.
The whole time I just kept

getting more irritated…

not only with everything
that had happened

but with these goddamn
shoelaces from hell.

I looked back to grab my shoe
and a kid held it

with his hands
and began to walk toward me.

He handed over my shoe.

"Thanks, man," I said.

"You're welcome," he replied.

We began to exchange words.

He was a smart kid,
a happy kid—worry free, too.

His face was shining—innocent
as if he hadn't felt the burn
of life.

He was sixteen,
maybe even seventeen.

He talked to me
with much enthusiasm about school,

about how much he was ready
to start college
and start his new life.

His eyes were bright
and full of life.

"Don't grow up too fast," I said.

"Enjoy your last few months
as a high schooler."

The sun was glistening
and the salt from the ocean
filled our lungs.

"I'm also getting transferred
and promoted as soon as I graduate,

so I can move with my mom.
My little brother has cancer," he said.

Shit, man!
And here I was
the whole time thinking

this kid had it good
and I had it bad.

"Cancer?"

"Yeah man, cancer,
but it's alright.
He'll be okay. I know it."

I took a moment to myself...
because it was a sad thing
to hear.

"I'm sorry to hear that, kid."

"Don't be...
we'll be alright.
I know he'll get better

but hey,
I have to go...
it was nice meeting you,"
he said, as he took off.

That day
I realized a few things.

1. The blessing of life
is your spirit
and if you lose it…
you lose everything.

2. Never judge anyone
by the way they talk, dress, walk, etc.

you never know
what kind of worry
people are carrying.

3. My problems
are so goddamn small
and sometimes
it takes an encounter like that
to realize this.

4. *Hope is a beautiful thing.*

5. The strongest people
in the world are children.

and

6. Cancer is a motherfucker
and sometimes
the good die young
and the young die a little harder

than any of

us

ever could.